Published by
Book Publishers Ink

For permission requests, please contact the publisher at the address above.

Acknowledgement

I just want to take a moment to thank each of you for the support, kindness, and encouragement you've shown me over the years. Through every high and low, your presence—whether in big ways or small—has made a difference in my life.

Life isn't always easy, but knowing I have people like you in my corner has given me the strength to keep pushing forward. Your support has meant more than words can express, and I'm truly grateful for the friendships and connections we've built.

No matter where life takes us, please know that I appreciate you and everything you've done. Thank you for being a part of my journey.

With gratitude,
Thomas Graves

And Then They Came

First, they came for the rivers and lands,
But I did not speak, for I had no plans.

Then they came for the books in the schools,
But I turned away—I followed no rules.

Then they came for the elders' due,
But it was not mine, so I let it pass through.

Then they came for those who had borne the fight,
But I was not one, so I thought it was right.

And then they came, their hands stretched wide,
No one remained to stand by my side

The Fall of the Corrupt

The halls of power glow with gold,
built on the backs of stories untold.
The cries of the many lost in the din,
as greed and ambition conspire to win.

They barter souls with whispered lies,
cast nations out, let truth demise.
A king's ransom for a traitor's cause,
justice delayed, a world on pause.

But grind they do, those wheels of fate,
unyielding hands that turn too late.
No coin can bribe, no voice can sway,
when reckoning comes to claim its day.

A name once feared, now cursed and torn,
a lesson learned, a warning worn.
Erased from ledgers, lost to time,
a mark of shame, a tarnished crime.

So feast today on stolen breath,
for soon you'll taste the dust of death.
The world may turn its gaze away,
but justice waits—it does not stray.

If This Is the Path

If this is what you truly need,
if this is what you truly want,
then I must step beyond the noise,
beyond the doubt, beyond the haunt.

I'll carve my name upon the winds,
make my mark in stone and sand,
embrace the weight of my own sins,
and hold my fate within my hand.

I'll seek the soul who sees my scars,
who reads my words and hears my song,
who finds my laughter in the dark
and knows with me is where they belong.

Someone to share the quiet nights,
the simple joys, the fleeting days,
who loves the things I bring to life,
who walks with me through fire and grace.

If this is what the journey means,
then I will walk it, strong and free.
Not just to love, but to be loved—
not just to dream, but to be seen.

Weathering Love's Storm

Don't worry, my love, we can weather the storm,
Through the thunder and rain,
I'll keep you warm.
The winds may howl, the skies may cry,
But side by side, we'll stand, you and I.

We will stand the test of time, strong and true,
Every trial, every tear, I'll face with you.
No force can shake what's built to last,
Our love will rise, unbound by the past.

I will love you till the stars fade away,
Till time itself forgets the day.
I'll be the man who never leaves,
The one who holds you when your heart grieves.

In despair, I'll be your light,
Your shelter in the darkest night.
With every heartbeat, I promise you,
Forever faithful, yours

For Liberty, I Stand

Once more, I go, where the fearless tread,
Not young, not old—just bound by thread
Of duty's call, of freedom's claim,
A spark still burning, a whispered name.

Regret? No, none—save one alone,
That I have but one life to atone,
To give, to rise, to take my place,
Against the chains, against disgrace.

March's wind will bear my cry,
Beneath the cold, unyielding sky.
With sons of liberty, I stand,
Against the weight of tyrant's hand.

I know not if I shall return,
If time will grant or fates will burn,
But should I fall, remember true,
I did this all for them—for you.

For peace, for honor, for those who dream,
For voices lost in silenced screams.
So if I go and don't come back,
Know I walked the righteous track.

In Every Dawn and Dusk

I wake you softly with a whispered kiss,
A gentle touch, a moment of bliss.
The morning light paints gold on your face,
And in your eyes, I find my place.

We share the warmth of coffee's embrace,
Steam curling slow like time's sweet trace.
The rising sun, a silent vow,
To love you deeper here and now.

Through fleeting hours and shifting skies,
I search for ways to mesmerize.
A touch, a glance, a love-made tune,
A dance beneath the silver moon.

And when the night pulls stars in tight,
I hold you close in grateful light.
Another day, another way,
To love you more than yesterday.

The clock face mocks, a frozen, cruel jest,
Each second stretches, an eternity's test.
The air grows thin, a phantom limb's ache,
A hollow echo where your presence should break.
The world's a muted canvas, colors drained,
A silent movie, where your voice is chained.
The sun, a cold disc, yields no warming grace,
Just empty hours, in this desolate space.
My thoughts, like restless birds, circle and fly,
Seeking the warmth of your nearness, nearby.
They weave a tapestry of moments we've known,
And whisper promises of when you'll be home.
This vast expanse, this aching, vacant void,
Is not despair, but a strength I've employed.
For every moment that your absence defines,
A fiercer longing, a love that intertwines.
Like desert flowers, thirsting for the rain,
My spirit waits, to bloom and rise again.
This endless stretch, this agonizing wait,
Will make our reunion a glorious fate.
So let the minutes crawl, the shadows grow deep,
My heart, a compass, your direction will keep.
For every second lost, a brighter day's gleam,
A love reborn, a waking, vibrant dream.

I Call It You

They call love a weight, a duty to bear,
a tether that binds, a cross to share.
Some play it like cards, a wager, a game,
never knowing its fire, only its name.

To the lonely, it's distant—a whisper, a dream,
a flicker of light on an unreachable stream.
To the wise, it's fate, a path carved in stone,
two souls entwined, forever known.

But love to me is none of these things,
not fate, nor duty, nor fleeting wings.
It is laughter in silence, warmth in the cold,
a story rewritten, a hand to hold.

It is the breath between words,
the calm in the storm,
the place I belong, the hearth that is warm.
Love is not distant, nor fickle, nor new—
Love has a name, and I call it you.

A House, Not a Home

These walls stand bare, hollow and gray,
void of color, void of light.
No laughter echoes in the empty halls,
no warmth lingers in the silent night.

The kitchen gathers dust, unused,
no scent of spice, no warmth of bread.
The walls hold no whispered stories,
no memories framed, no love once said.

A house, it is—but not a home,
until your voice filled the air.
Until your hands wove warmth in shadows,
until your laughter settled there.

Now, the walls glow with your presence,
the silence hums with something new.
Love has painted what time had stolen—
this house, at last, is home with you.

A hush descends, a sudden, soft eclipse,
When beauty's current flows from your sweet lips.
No crafted word, no poet's gilded phrase,
Can capture the wonder of your sunlit gaze.
My tongue, a traitor, stumbles, finds no sound,
Where eloquence should flourish, I'm unbound.
For how to speak of starlight in your hair,
Or the gentle curve, the grace you always wear?
Your skin, a canvas, warm beneath my hand,
A whispered secret, I can barely stand.
A silken whisper, where my fingers trace,
A map of heaven, etched upon your face.
And then, the stolen kiss, a fragile, bright spark,
Igniting wildfires, hidden in the dark.
A breathless moment, where all time suspends,
And every sense, to your sweet presence, bends.
The thrill, a tremor, deep within my soul,
A tidal wave, that takes complete control.
It leaves me anchored, in a tranquil sea,
Where only you, and your pure beauty, be.
No need for language, no elaborate art,
Your simple presence, tears my world apart.
And in that silence, where all words take flight,
I find a solace, bathed in your soft light

Minefield of Love

I step with care, my heart in hand,
Through fields of longing, shifting sand.
Each pretty face—a hidden snare,
A whispered promise, a fleeting glare.

Words explode in double light,
Soft in tone, but laced with fight.
Do you mean love, or just the game?
Another spark, another flame.

I chase salvation, something real,
A touch, a bond, a love to feel.
Yet every turn, another trial,
Another ghost, another mile.

But I will walk, though bruised and worn,
Through love's cruel field—betrayed, reborn.
For somewhere past this endless test,
Awaits the heart that beats the best.

All That I Have, I Give to You

If kisses were water, I'd flood the sky,
let oceans rise where your lips lie.
Tides would dance to your gentle call,
endless waves—I'd give you them all.

If hugs were leaves, the trees would grow,
a forest deep where love would show.
Branches strong, their roots so true,
every leaf would reach for you.

If love were space, the stars would shine,
a galaxy bright that is wholly mine.
Planets would turn in endless embrace,
caught in the pull of your gentle grace.

If friendship were life, no price I'd see,
for all I am, I'd give for free.
No breath too great, no step too far,
for you, my heart, my guiding star.

More Than Poetry
(Part 1)

Her last words to me—
"I hope your next woman likes poetry,"
as if rhyme and verse are all I am,
as if love is only written, not lived.

Before her, I was more—
a husband, a father, a builder of dreams.
I started as a summer temp,
worked my hands to the bone,
rose to an engineer, crafting a future
with sweat, with fire, with heart.

So no, I do not hope my next love enjoys poetry.
I hope she enjoys me.

I hope she loves the flowers I bring,
not for occasion, but simply because.
I hope she savors the chocolate, the surprises,
the small gifts tucked between moments.

More Than Poetry
(Part 11)

I hope she sings that song when
she thinks no one hears,
and smiles when I hum along.
I hope she laughs at the glue in her coffee,
stirs it slow just because she can.

I hope she runs where the road has no name,
finds adventure in the quiet,
lays beside me, breath against breath,
as we count the stars in a sky that
belongs to no one.

I hope she cherishes warm kisses in passing,
random hugs that hold more than arms ever could.
I hope she sees that love is not just words,
not just poetry—
but something built, something lived,

something real.

Ode to the Goddess of War

I crawl, hands bloodied, knees torn,
A supplicant at the altar of your wrath.
Your name is carved into the marrow of my bones,
A whisper that ignites like flint on steel.

Time falters, crumbles to dust,
Yet my devotion stands unshaken,
A pillar in the storm of your conquest,
A shadow stretching endless in your wake.

I bring you flame, the scent of sacrifice,
Ash curling into the darkened sky—
A burnt offering, the last of my worth,
To prove that I was ever yours.

Take me, break me, shape me anew,
Let my body be the armor at your feet.
For love is war, and war is you,
And I am lost, eternally bound.

Do Not Mistake Me

If it comes to war, I will not waver,
steel in my spine, fire in my hands.
I have bled before—more than I care to count—
and if you test me, it will not be the last.

I have given, I have knelt,
offered my kindness as an open palm,
but do not mistake it for weakness,
for there is iron beneath this skin.

I would lay down my life, not for glory,
but for love, for justice, for you.
I would stand between you and the dark,
shatter my body to keep you whole.

I do not seek war, but I do not fear it.
I have seen blood soak the earth,
felt the weight of choices carved in bone—
and I have made peace with my rage.
So take heed—
this heart is open, but ut these hands are ready.

The Song Remains

Your song comes on, soft and slow,
And my heart knows before my mind.
My knee aches, my chest goes tight,
Like time itself is rewinding.

I try to turn away, to breathe,
But every note pulls me back in.
Down the road where laughter lived,
Before love turned to what-could-have-beens.

Can't she hear she's tearing me open,
Spinning me through what's long been gone?
Doesn't she know this melody aches,
A ghost that lingers in every song?

Before the silence, before the fall,
Before our hearts forgot to beat—
There was music, there was us,
Now just echoes on repeat.

Yours, Always

I don't want maybe, I don't want someday,
I want forever, I want always.
Not a fleeting touch, not a passing glance,
But a love that grips, a love that stands.

I want to kiss you breathless, deep,
To be the reason you lose sleep.
To hold you close when the world spins fast,
To be the first, to be the last.

I don't want games, I don't want space,
I want your heart, your time, your grace.
To be the reason you turn down plans,
The one you reach for, hand in hand.

I'll be your anchor, your steady ground,
The love you run to, safe and sound.
So let me in, don't be afraid,
I'll lock you down in love that stays.

All That I Am, I Give to You

If kisses were water, I'd bring you the sea,
waves that whisper your name endlessly.
A tide that rises, fierce and true,
crashing, flowing—forever to you.

If hugs were leaves, I'd give you a wood,
a forest where love forever stood.
Roots entwined, strong and deep,
a place where hearts and souls would keep.

If love were space, I'd paint the skies,
scatter stars like fire in your eyes.
A universe vast, no end in sight,
spinning for you in endless light.

If friendship were life, then take mine whole,
no second thought, no shattered soul.
For all I am, and all I do,
is nothing, love, if not for you.

Haunted

Sometimes, I miss you in the quiet spaces,
Where your laughter used to live.
Other times, you slip into my dreams,
Leaving echoes I can't forgive.

Some days, you walk through my thoughts,
Uninvited, yet impossible to ignore.
I catch your scent in the empty air,
Like you're still lingering by the door.

Sometimes, there's a ghost of us,
Fading, yet refusing to fade.
A love that left but never left,
A shadow I can't escape.

More Than Enough

I was never searching for gold,
Not a balance sheet, not riches untold.
I didn't need a present wrapped in a bow,
Just a love that stays, a hand to hold.

I've been broken, I've been torn,
Wings too heavy, dreams too worn.
But I never asked for wealth or fame,
Just someone who'd whisper my name—
Like it was a promise, like it was safe,
Like love was more than a fleeting embrace.

I wanted arms to steady the fall,
Not a ledger, not a debt to recall.
Someone to sit through the quietest nights,
Not just the highs, but the long, uphill fights.

I only wanted to be seen,
To love, to trust, to be believed.
To heal these wings, to rise once more,
To fly beside the one I adore.

Love Across the Distance

I make love to you with my poetry,
each word pulling you closer,
wrapping around you like whispered heat,
keeping you safe in the arms of my verse.

My lines trace your lips,
keeping them soft, longing,
pressing kisses between the spaces
where miles try to keep us apart.

I devour you in every way possible,
not with touch, but with thought,
not with hands, but with longing,
not with presence, but with poetry—
the only thing that can reach you now.

And though the distance stands between us,
though my arms ache for the weight of you,
know this—
I am the one you need,
and my love, like these words,
will always find its way to you.

Eternal Love

Roses wither, their petals fall,
chocolates melt, their sweetness fades.
Diamonds, though brilliant, still hold flaws,
but my love for you—unchanging,
unwavering—remains.

It never dulls, never breaks,
never bends beneath the weight of time.
It does not spoil, does not stain,
does not falter in the darkest night.

Seasons may shift, the world may change,
but my love is carved in something deeper,
etched into forever itself.
No cracks, no doubts, no end—
only us, only always.

Happy Birthday, My Love

Happy birthday, baby,
the light in my days, the warmth in my nights.
Happy birthday, my sweet,
the melody my heart sings when
the world is quiet.

Happy birthday, love of my life,
the one who makes every moment shine,
who turns the ordinary into something divine.
Happy birthday, my sweet angel,
the soul I cherish, the dream I live.

May your day be as beautiful as you,
may your heart be as full as the love I hold for you.
Today, tomorrow, always—
you are my greatest gift.

Diamond in Our Eyes

That's a pretty diamond—do you know what it means?
Not just love, not just devotion,
but the faith we have in you,
the fire we see burning beneath your skin.

It means we believe—
that you will carve your name into the world,
that your hands will shape the future,
that your steps will leave echoes long after you're gone.

It doesn't mean we'll never falter,
that we'll always be faithful,
that we'll walk without missteps.
But it means, in our eyes,
there is nothing more perfect than you.

You are brilliance, uncut and unbreakable,
a force that will change everything,
not for power, not for pride,
but for good.

Hidden in Plain Sight

I was your jewel, tucked in the quiet,
a whisper among the noise,
a steady pulse beneath your skin,
offering without demand.

I asked for nothing,
but to worship—
the curve of your body,
the fire in your mind,
the echoes of your soul.

You were a storm, I was the rain,
falling freely into your world,
drenching you in devotion,
without ever asking if you noticed.

May you feel more than whole,
even if my hands no longer hold you,
even if my love remains unseen,
a light forever hidden—
but always shining.

Ghost of Us

You turn your back, but I stand still,
Silent shadow, bending will.
Your choice is made, the past is done,
Yet I remain—I do not run.

If flowers wilted in your hands,
If rings were lost like shifting sands,
Then let them fade, let them decay,
But what we had won't drift away.

The roads we walked, the skies we knew,
The places where the wild wind blew—
They stay with me, they whisper low,
Echoes of a love let go.

No blade of loss can cut too deep,
No ghost of us will steal my sleep.
I move ahead, my path is clear,
With lessons learned, but without fear.

Boundless Heart

Love knows no borders, no drawn lines,
It's the quiet truth that our souls define.
Beyond the hues of skin and light,
Our hearts entwine in a dance so bright.

In a realm where limits fade away,
Love is the pulse that refuses to stray.
It sings in whispers, fierce and true,
A melody of me, a resonance of you.

No barrier can shackle this fervent art—
For love is the language of one boundless heart.
Unconfined, uncolored, pure in every part,
It bridges the distances, making us whole from
the start.

Missing You Before I Knew You

I would miss you even if I hadn't met you,
like a song I've never heard but somehow hum,
a shadow cast before the dawn,
a whisper of warmth in the coldest sun.

My world would not seem complete,
like a puzzle with its final piece misplaced,
a road that bends but never meets,
a story paused in empty space.

Every breath would be lacking,
as if the air forgot its dance,
each inhale tinged with longing,
each exhale a lost romance.

Showers would never quite be hot enough,
steam rising but never embracing,
like love that lingers just out of reach,
like fingertips barely tracing.

And yet, though I haven't found you,
I know you're somewhere near,
written in the stars, etched in the tide,
pulling me closer, year by year.

Fractured Land

We once were hands clasped in promise,
A chorus of voices, rising as one.
A nation built on hope and difference,
Bound not by blood, but by belief.

Once, the colors blended freely,
A melting pot of dream and dust.
Now they split like oil on water,
Drifting further with each gust.

Majority presses upon minority,
Minority turns upon the next—
Lines are drawn, voices sharpened,
Does division ever rest?

We speak of unity, yet build our walls,
We preach of love, yet cast our stones.
Is there a bridge beyond the breaking?
A place where kindness still belongs?

Or will we drown in all this anger,
Lost in echoes of the past,
Forgetting that we rose together,
And only together do we last?

Whispered Surrender

"Yes," she breathed, soft and low,
A spark that set his blood to glow.
A single word, yet laced with fire,
Unraveling threads of raw desire.

He pulled her close, fierce and tight,
Fingertips tracing heat and light.
No space remained, no air, no sound,
Just bodies speaking, lost and found.

He showed her love not softly spun,
But burning bright, a rising sun.
No hesitation, no retreat,
Just whispered pleas and tangled sheets.

She knew, at last, in every breath,
What it meant to lose herself to death—
Not of life, but of control,
To be reborn in something whole.

Moscato Dreams

Your green eyes close, soft as whispers in the night,
Hand poised, lifting the glass, a tender delight.
The Moscato kisses your lips, sweet and slow,
A river of ambrosia, letting desire flow.

Your hair cascades, a silk curtain in the air,
Sinking into the water, releasing each care.
Bubbles rise and burst against your skin's glow,
Tiny sparks of pleasure only you could know.

Can fate explain how our paths intertwined?
The meeting of souls, the merging of minds.
The scent of your essence, a fragrant embrace,
The taste of your lips—pure passion, no trace.

Wine dances over your teeth, a teasing flame,
Its warmth ignites you, a lover's game.
The liquid heat courses, your body alive,
A rush of desire, too fierce to survive.

Your thoughts swim deep in the sea of might-be,
Consumed by the pulse of sweet possibility.
Where could this lead? Let the question remain—
A journey of fire, both pleasure and pain.

Our Story
(Part 1)

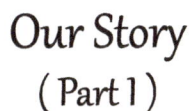

Our story begins where the sun meets the sea,
In whispers of winds and the roots of the tree.
Each thread in the weave, a memory spun,
A journey together, a tale just begun.

Through rivers of laughter and
mountains of tears,
We built this bridge across our years.
With hands entwined and hearts ablaze,
We crafted love in countless ways.

The storms have roared; the skies have wept,
Yet promises made were promises kept.
Our story endures, in ink and air,
In shadows and sunlight, everywhere.

For it's not just words, nor chapters alone,
But the spaces between, where seeds are sown.
In the quiet of night, in the break of dawn,
Our story sings, and forever lives on.

Our Story
(Part 11)

I am an ally, a patriot, a friend,
A quiet constant that will not bend.
In silence, I stand as you speak your truth,
Through age and time, from the days of youth.

I celebrate with you in moments of cheer,
A steadfast presence when joy feels near.
I step to the front when the burden is great,
A harbor of peace when you challenge your fate.

Silent reverence, I give when you choose,
Your voice the beacon, your path to pursue.
From the Underground Railroad to the labor fight,
I've stood in the shadows, shunning the light.

Through the sweep of history, I've held my ground,
An unnamed force, in whispers profound.
No monuments bear the weight of my name,
But in your freedom, I stake my claim.

The Scales Must Balance

"Enough," he said, as the silence broke,
The time for shadows has gone up in smoke.
I've stood too long with my head turned away,
But justice calls; we must answer today.

We are a land built on sacred laws,
A place where freedom has righteous cause.
Not bent by gold, not swayed by greed,
But bound to the truth in word and deed.

One vote, one voice, for all to proclaim,
Not sold to power, not tarnished by blame.
Not you, not her, not any man,
Will trample the rights this country began.

The scales must balance, the truth must weigh,
We cannot let justice decay.
For when the mighty silence the weak,
The soul of a nation begins to creak.

Stand now, for the hour grows late,
Let us rebuild, let us elevate.
Together, as one, we'll right the wrongs,
For justice lives where the brave belong.

The Price of Truth
(Part 1)

America, you sang of liberty,
Taught us dreams of equality,
Yet the scales of justice tilt and sway,
For those with gold to pave their way.

The rich don't answer, they simply evade,
A fortress of wealth their justice brigade.
While lies and deceit make their ascent,
The people's faith cracks, twisted, bent.

The playground of power, a ruthless game,
Where honor and virtue are hollow names.
They cheer the corrupt, ignore the plight,
Of those who struggle to claim their right.

The Price of Truth
(Part 11)

Truth is a treasure, but now it seems,
It's auctioned off, sold in shattered dreams.
What happened to the ideals we knew,
The promise of fairness, bold and true?

America, your star still shines,
But its light feels dimmed by greed's confines.
Yet in the shadows, hope might rise,
A voice of change beneath the skies.

For justice can't forever sleep,
Its roots run strong, its roots run deep.
Perhaps one day the tide will turn,
And hearts will wake, and justice burn.

Hidden in Plain Sight

I was your jewel, tucked in the quiet,
a whisper among the noise,
a steady pulse beneath your skin,
offering without demand.

I asked for nothing,
but to worship—
the curve of your body,
the fire in your mind,
the echoes of your soul.

You were a storm, I was the rain,
falling freely into your world,
drenching you in devotion,
without ever asking if you noticed.

May you feel more than whole,
even if my hands no longer hold you,
even if my love remains unseen,
a light forever hidden—
but always

The Ghost of Us

I put up the chocolates you'll never eat,
tucked them away like a fading dream.
The sweetness has turned into silence now,
melting away at the seams.

I set out the ring you'll never wear,
its shimmer now dull in the light.
A promise that never found fingers to hold,
a whisper lost deep in the night.

I watched the roses wilt and die,
petal by petal, they fell.
Like echoes of laughter that once filled this room,
now only the emptiness swells.

I gather the things you left behind,
folding the past into place.
Yet no matter how much I try to let go,
I still feel the ghost of your face.

More Than Unrequited

It took her leaving for me to see,
I am worth more than what she gave to me.
More than the silence, more than the ache,
More than the love she refused to make.

I begged, I pleaded, I lost my pride,
Hoping she'd stay, stand by my side.
But love should never be a fight,
A one-way struggle in the dead of night.

I poured my soul, but it wasn't enough,
She weighed my heart and found it rough.
Yet now I stand, no less, no small—
I was always worth it after all.

Boundaries

I won't tread where I'm not wanted,
Nor claim what's not mine to hold.
Why does this confuse so many,
When respect is worth more than gold?

"Your body, my choice"—a hollow phrase,
A lie that shatters trust and peace.
Without respect for others' rights,
Your own desires must surely cease.

To take from others what is theirs,
Without consent, without regard,
Is to forfeit your own humanity,
Leaving both souls deeply scarred.

So honor boundaries, honor choice,
Let respect be your guiding light.
For only then can we all share
A world where wrong is turned to right.

A Journey Through Words: My Path to Poetry

A Journey Through Words: My Path to Poetry

Life has a way of leading us to unexpected places. For me, it all began with a freak accident—one that left me temporarily blind. In that darkness, I discovered something that would stay with me for a lifetime: a love for poetry.

Words became my vision, my way of processing the world when I couldn't see it. What started as an outlet soon became a passion, and over the years, poetry turned into my voice—my way of expressing love, resilience, and the emotions that connect us all.

Now, I'm taking a leap of faith. Stepping out and publishing my poetry isn't just about sharing my work—it's about creating connections with like-minded people who feel the depth of words the way I do. Through my writing, I hope to communicate the love, struggle, and beauty that shape our lives.

To everyone who has supported me on this journey, thank you. This is just the beginning, and I'm excited to share my words with the world.

Stay connected, stay inspired, and always embrace the power of expression.

Thomas Graves

www.ingramcontent.com/pod-product-compliance
Lightning Source LLC
Chambersburg PA
CBHW051337120626
46547CB00016B/2579